THE JOY OF WINE

THE JOY OF WINE

JANE HUGHES

LORENZ BOOKS

This edition published by Lorenz Books
an imprint of
Anness Publishing Limited
Hermes House
88-89 Blackfriars Road
London SE1 8HA

Published in the USA by Lorenz Books
Anness Publishing Inc., 27 West 20th Street, New York, NY 10011;
(800) 354-9657

This edition distributed in Canada by Raincoast Books
8680 Cambie Street, Vancouver, British Columbia V6P 6M9

A CIP catalogue record for this book is available from the British Library

Publisher: Joanna Lorenz
Project Editor: Joanne Rippin
Designers: Prue Bucknall and Ruth Prentice
Photography by: Steven Baxter, Michelle Garrett and Amanda Heywood
Jacket Design: Wilson Harvey Marketing and Design

Previously published as *The Wine-Lover's Guide*

© Anness Publishing Limited 1997
Updated © 2000
1 3 5 7 9 10 8 6 4 2

PICTURE ACKNOWLEDGEMENTS

The publishers would like to thank the following people and
organizations for providing additional pictures for the book.
Bridgeman Art Library: pp 20, 31, 41, 47, 48, 51.
Cephas Picture Library: pp 6, 18r, 19, 24r, 26r, 27, 28r, 30l, 30r, 33, 34, 35, 36l, 38l, 38r, 37r, 40, 42, 43, 44,
45, 46r, 49, 53, 54.
Fine Art Photographic: pp 32l, 36–37, 46l, 55.
German Wine Institute: p 18l. Italian Trade Centre: pp 22l, 22r, 23.
Sopexa: pp 26l, 28l, 34br, 42r, 56r.
Visual Arts Library: pp 8, 9, 10, 12l, 12r, 13, 14l, 14r, 15, 16l, 16r,
17, 21, 24l, 29, 39, 52, 57. Wines of Chile: p 25.
(l=left, r=right, b=bottom, t=top)

PAGE 2: The Drinkers *by Velasquez* (1629)
PAGE 3: *A front page illustration from a 1911 edition of the French magazine* Le Petit Journal, *depicting the harvest festivities of the local winegrowers.*

CONTENTS

INTRODUCTION

If you think wine appreciation is the domain of the pompous or snobbish, think again. Yes, wine does have its mystery and romance, but these just add to its charms.

Every year, in different parts of the world, there are new wines being made, from the very grandest to the everyday. Take a look and you'll find there's something for everyone, just waiting to be discovered. It doesn't have to be expensive to be exciting, nor does it have to be shrouded in technical terms to taste good.

The intention of this book is to introduce you, albeit briefly, to this fascinating and exciting subject. It will be identifying some of the major wine styles, explaining the basics of winemaking, and suggesting ways to help you gain the most pleasure out of every glass. Hopefully, if you have not already begun your own love affair with wine, this book will encourage you to do so.

LEFT: *The magic of Champagne – row upon row of bottles of fizz in the underground cellars, held in traditional wooden pupitres.*

CHAPTER 1

THE
HISTORY
OF
WINE

LEFT: *The vintage at Château Lagrange, by J. Breton, 1864.*

ABOVE: *A fifteenth-century harvest, illustrated in the Codice Forli, Biblioteca Communale.*

THE
CLASSICAL AGE

Wine drinking has been traced back through thousands of years to its roots in the Middle East. Early in 1996 a container was found on an architectural site in northern Iran that contained traces of fermented juice, thought to be the earliest form of wine. The pot dates from the Stone Age, around 5000 BC.

We know too that wine played a role in the Ancient Egyptian civilization: scenes painted on surviving pottery depict arbours of vines and people carrying jugs of wine. That wine was an important part of daily life so long ago is reinforced by the numerous references to it in the Bible. Wine, "the blood of grapes", is used as a powerful metaphor for life; and the Old Testament tells the story of how Noah planted a vineyard and made wine.

As winemaking gradually spread from its birthplace, through Egypt, and to the west and south, it was embraced by the Ancient Greeks and became central to their sense of civilized living. Counted among the Greek gods was the beautiful youth, Dionysus, the god of wine, who wore a crown of vine leaves.

ANCIENT GREECE AND ROME
As they travelled and traded overseas, the Ancient Greeks took with them the vine and the idea of wine production. It was the trade

between the Greeks – who named southern Italy "Enotria", meaning "the land of vines" – and Romans from around the first century AD that marked the beginning of vine cultivation throughout Europe. The poet Virgil recorded possibly the earliest references to the vagaries of vintages, and described the winemaking methods used by the Romans.

By the end of the fifth century AD, the Romans had created what are still the world's most renowned vineyard areas: Bordeaux, Burgundy, the Rhône, the Loire, and the Moselle and Rhine valleys of Germany. The key was the major river routes these regions lay on – offering an easy means of transporting the barrels (which had replaced the clay amphorae used by the Greeks).

By this time, however, the Roman Empire was collapsing, and with it went the market for "fine" wine. Through the Dark Ages that followed, it was the Church that became the focus of winemaking throughout Europe.

TOP LEFT: Grapes are harvested from the vine in this detail from an Ancient Egyptian wall painting.

ABOVE: "Les Amours", a frieze from the ruins of Pompeii. Wine is poured from the amphora into a tastevin.

EARTH IS BOUNTEOUS
AND FOR MY PEOPLE
TOO, IT BRINGS FORTH
GRAPES THAT THRIVE
ON THE RAIN OF ZEUS
AND THAT MAKE
GOOD WINE, BUT THIS
IS DISTILLED INTO
NECTAR AND
AMBROSIA.
Homer
The Odyssey

RIGHT: *An illuminated*
manuscript showing the
saints harvesting grapes in
the revelation to Beatus
de Liebana.

11

WINE IN MEDIEVAL EUROPE

WINE IS A TURNCOAT
– FIRST A FRIEND,
THEN AN ENEMY.
George Herbert
(1593–1633)

By the twelfth century most of the great vineyards of France and Germany were owned by the monasteries of the powerful Benedictine and Cistercian orders. The Cistercian order, which was based in Burgundy's Côte d'Or, created the still-famous Clos de Vougeot vineyard, and later Kloster Eberbach in Germany.

The rise of Italy as the centre of commerce from the eleventh century, wars and royal marriages between the English, French and German nobility, and the power of the Church – all these factors played a role in the ownership of vineyards and the creation of markets for wine well into the Middle Ages. The repute of Burgundian wines was spread by the Roman Church, and supported by the Valois dukes who ruled much of the region until the late 1400s. Bordeaux in particular benefited from strong commercial links with Britain, where wine, ale, or mead – made from fermented honey – were everyday drinks. Shakespeare's Falstaff would regularly call for sack, a fortified wine, in the taverns of London.

ENTER THE BOTTLE

Wine was sold, and served, very young (while it was still drinkable). It was acidic and probably very rough. It was stored in barrels that sped up

FAR LEFT: *Treading the grapes in fourteenth-century Italy.*

RIGHT: *Images of vines and winemaking became a favourite subject-matter for religious illuminated manuscripts. This twelfth-century harvest is taken from the pages of the Hunterian Psalter.*

FAR RIGHT: *Published in 1513, this German engraving was entitled "The Soul of Wine".*

the oxidation of the wine. The major breakthrough, and the beginnings of wine that we might recognize, came in the early 1700s. An English manufacturer developed a glass of a quality good enough to make sturdy bottles, and it was not long before the practice of sealing the bottles with stoppers became universal. This seemed to improve the wine, or at least keep it palatable for longer.

Vins de garde – wines produced specifically for ageing – were introduced, led by two French wine regions, Bordeaux and Burgundy. These "reserve" wines commanded a better price, something which hasn't changed to this day.

EVOLUTION AND REVOLUTION

Different styles of wines began to evolve, some by accident and others by design. Champagne was originally a high-acid, still wine which had a tendency to develop bubbles in the spring or summer after it was made. (Cold winters stopped fermentation early; when the weather warmed up, fermentation would re-start, giving off carbon dioxide.) This "sparkling" wine became quite the thing in the frivolous café societies of the 1720s. With the advent of bottles that were strong enough to withstand the pressure created by the trapped "bubbles" of carbonic gas, Champagne became an accepted, frothy style of wine.

France and Britain traded freely enough in times of peace, but war forced merchants to look elsewhere for wines. From the late 1600s onwards commerce gradually built up with the Portuguese. It was at this time that British merchants discovered a red wine made by an abbot in Portugal's Douro Valley. It was unusual in that it was slightly sweet, because he added a little grape brandy *before* the wine finished fermenting.

FORTIFYING WINES

Adding brandy to wine was not a novelty. The only way to ship wines without turning them to vinegar had been to add grape brandy, to "fortify" them for the journey, but it was normally added well after fermentation had finished. This changed in 1730, when the abbot's example was copied deliberately, and a sweet, alcoholic red wine called port was introduced in England.

The French Revolution of 1780 impacted on the wine industry as forcefully as it did on all French life. The vineyards were taken from the Church and the nobility and auctioned back to the citizens. Vineyards were further divided by the Napoleonic law of inheritance that decreed all children should inherit equally. The legacy of these events can still be found today in the tiny plots of vines that make up much of Burgundy's famous vineyards.

FAR LEFT: *The grape harvest came to epitomise an ideal of the rustic way of life.*

LEFT: *By training vines on frames or trellises, growers can alter the way the fruit ripens.*

RIGHT: *"La Jeune Vendangeuse", painted by Caballero (1867-1951), returns with baskets laden with fruit.*

SPREADING THE WORD

By the nineteenth century, the wine market was booming. There was Burgundy, Bordeaux, Champagne, sherry, port, and "Hock" from Germany. But they were still not wines that we would necessarily recognize by those names today. Hock was high in acid, brownish in colour and aged in character – strikingly different to the delicate perfumed, white and often off-dry wines for which Germany is renowned.

There were two sweet wines that dominated the tables of the wealthy of Europe: the botrytised Tokaji of Hungary, and Constantia, a sweet Muscat that came from South Africa.

THE NEW WORLD

While Europe's wine boom was going on, the vine had been spreading beyond Europe, or the "Old World", to new continents, carried by monks and pilgrims, explorers and emigrants. Vines were carried to Mexico by the Spanish as early as 1519, and on down into Chile, while Jesuit missionaries introduced vines to Argentina in the mid-1500s.

The Dutch Jan van Riebeeck shipped cuttings from French vines and established the first vineyards on South Africa's Cape in the 1650s. The arrival of the Protestant Huguenots ensured the establishment of quality wine-growing in the Cape region, and in 1685 the world-renowned Constantia estate was established.

It was via the Cape that the first vines arrived in Australia in the 1780s. However, it was not until a 24-year-old viticulturist, James Busby, arrived in Australia from Scotland with a grant to plant a vineyard in the Hunter Valley, that wine-making across much of south-eastern Australia really took off.

North American winemaking began when Spaniards planted a grape variety called Mission in Texas in the middle of the 1600s. Vines were planted across north America in the following centuries, and by the end of the 1800s New York State dominated wine production. Today, the sunshine state of California is the country's major wine-producing state. It was the gold rush of the mid-1800s that drew people to northern California, and introduced the "noble" grapes of Europe to the state.

FAR LEFT: *The international trade in wine begins to boom.*

LEFT: *"Autumn and the Harvest", painted by Goya in 1787.*

RIGHT: *"Grape Pickers in the French Countryside", by Pierre de Chavannes.*

GOD MADE ONLY WATER, BUT MAN MADE WINE.
Victor Hugo
(1802–1885)

MODERN WINEMAKING

While vines were shipped from Europe to North America, a vicious vine pest was brought back to Europe. The signs began in France in the 1860s, where the precious grape vines began to die off. The louse, known as phylloxera, attacked the roots of the *Vitis vinifera* vine, the species used to grow wine grapes. The disease quickly spread, sweeping through much of Europe's vineyards and destroying every vine in its path.

Growers thought they found the solution with an American rootstock, *Vitis rupestris*, which was immune to phylloxera. Unfortunately, its grapes gave a "foxy" flavour to the wine. Eventually the solution was discovered of grafting *vinifera* vines on to the rupestris rootstock, developing phylloxera-resistant vines that produced good fruit.

At the time the disease was a disaster, but the outcome has formed the basis on which modern vine-growing is founded. The scourge of phylloxera weeded out second-rate vineyards, and increased growers' understanding of the importance of quality vines and the need for good viticulture. However costly and time-consuming, grafting is vital. Only Chile, and a pocket of sandy vineyards in southern France, seem immune to the disease which remains a constant threat.

The twentieth century has witnessed a series of great leaps forward. Wines are now being made in South and North America, North Africa and the Middle East, and even China, while vineyards stretch across Europe from Russia to the island of Madeira. The last 30 years have also brought dramatic advances in winemaking technology and skills, and in our understanding of the vine and the grape, as science, technology, markets and regions have developed.

Those hundreds of thousands of vineyards, large and small, produce a myriad of styles, flavours, colours and aromas. Never has there been such an exciting array of wines on offer as there is today.

FAR LEFT: *A vineyard worker carefully tends his vines.*

ABOVE AND RIGHT: *The old world and the new. Vineyards in Monbazillac (above) south-west France, owned by the local co-operative, contrast with New Zealand's striking modern architecture (right) among Cabernet Sauvignon vines in Hawkes Bay.*

CHAPTER 2

FROM THE
VINEYARD
TO THE
CELLAR

ABOVE: *Wine merchants sample the newly-arrived barrels of wine at the docks in nineteenth-century London.*

LEFT: *A seventeenth-century still life by Jan van Kessel showing bottles of wine standing in a cooler.*

IN THE
VINEYARD

First there's the vine. Then there's the soil it is planted in, and then the weather during the year as the grapes grow and ripen. Once the human hand has done its part, it is then a question of time.

There are innumerable vine varieties, of which the *Vitis vinifera* (vine of the wine) is the species used in wine grape growing. The key to the success of *Vitis vinifera* grapes is their generally high sugar content, which turns to that magical alcohol during fermentation.

Vitis vinifera produces a wide range of grapes, thin or thick-skinned, ranging in colour from green to red to black, and in taste from bland to richly flavoured. Of the several hundred varieties grown, a mere dozen or so are considered the finest, or "noble" grapes, producing the most pleasurable wines. These include Chardonnay and Cabernet Sauvignon.

VINEYARDS AROUND THE WORLD

If you take a map of the world and mark where the vineyards mainly lie, you'll see they form a pair of bands around the globe between 30° and 50° latitude in each hemisphere. These bands offer the best balance of sun and rain, heat and cold, that allows the vines to grow and the grapes to ripen sufficiently.

THE IDEAL CONDITIONS
FOR VINES

❖ Cold winters so the vine can hibernate and store up strength for the following year's fruit.

❖ A long, warm summer, with some rain, so the fruit ripens slowly and evenly.

❖ A dry autumn for harvesting. If grapes take in too much water, the juice is diluted, losing that ripe flavour.

Where you decide to plant vines has an enormous effect on the quality and characteristics of the grape. The hot, arid plains of central Australia or the cold, wet climes of northern England are not ideal, but there are ways of making the most of what you have to hand.

FAR LEFT: *A beautiful bunch of green grapes on the vine, just ready for harvest.*

ABOVE: *Vines laden with ripe, heavy bunches of Trebbiano grapes, grown in abundance in Emilia-Romagna, east-central Italy.*

RIGHT: *A newly planted vineyard in Italy. The neat rows of young vines stretch across the sloping hillside.*

CULTIVATION
AND
HARVEST

In cool countries such as Germany, every available slope that faces south is covered with vines to catch as much sun as possible. The vines are also trained and pruned accordingly. Keeping the amount of foliage down ensures the grapes enjoy as much direct sunlight as possible. In hot areas of Australia, by contrast, keeping a canopy of foliage protects the grapes from "cooking" in too much sun.

The low-trained "bush" vines of France's Châteauneuf-du-Pape area benefit from the reflected heat from the stony soil found there, which helps ripen the grapes fully. In Chile and Argentina, vines are often trained on tall trellises, keeping the grapes high above the hot earth, and allowing air to circulate and cool them off.

Fertile soils make life too easy for the vine: it produces lush green foliage, which is not what the grower wants. Instead the vine is deliberately kept under stress, struggling in poorer soils, so that it will put all its energy into producing fruit.

Certain grapes benefit from particular soil types. Flinty soils are ideal for Rieslings, the lime-stone soils of Champagne and Chablis in France flatter the Chardonnay grape, while the "terra rossa" soil of Australia's Coonawarra district is the perfect site for fine Cabernet Sauvignon.

HARVEST TIME

It may come as no surprise that machine-harvesters are commonly used today. They are certainly ideal in the flat, sweeping vineyards of Australia, California and New Zealand, for example. Harvesting is quick, and can be done at night when the grapes are cool.

But picking is still done by hand all over the world. It is time-consuming, costly and back-breaking work, but it makes sense in small plots, and on the steep, rocky terrain of regions like Madeira and Portugal. And there's the quality of the grapes to be considered. They tend to be less damaged when picked by hand than when shaken from the vine by machine; unripe or rotten grapes can be left on the vine. In Burgundy's top vineyards, for example, pickers may go through the same vineyard several times, selecting only the grapes that are perfectly ripe.

FAR LEFT: *A sixteenth-century calendar depicts the October grape harvest. All the different stages of wine production are shown while a merchant samples the produce.*

BELOW: *It's back-breaking, hot work, picking grapes. These Nebbiolo grapes are destined for the fine red wine of Piedmont, Barolo.*

RIGHT: *Evening light falls on the vines in Chile's northerly Casablanca region, and picks out the distant Andes.*

WHITE GRAPE VARIETIES

The skins of the majority of grapes that are used for white wine can be anything from green to yellow, even pink. But their juice is pale, and the wine they then make is "white".

CHARDONNAY

The golden Chardonnay is a highly versatile variety. It appears in its traditional forms as Chablis – light, acid, appley, and unoaked – and as the classic oaked white Burgundy, with creamy, nutty oak and elegant fruit. In New Zealand it transforms into mouthwatering, crisply tropical-fruity, often unoaked wines; and in the hotter regions of Australia and California, home of the full-blown oaked Chardonnay, there's rich, luscious fruit, packed with vanilla and butter. It is also the vital ingredient in Champagne and much sparkling wine.

SAUVIGNON BLANC

In the cool Loire regions of Sancerre and Pouilly-Fumé, Sauvignon is crisply acid, grassy, at its best showing that famous "cat's pee" aroma and gooseberry character, and perhaps a hint of smoke. In Bordeaux's dry whites, it's softer, sometimes oaked to give a richer fruit style, and is added to the sweet wines of Sauternes to give them delicious tangy acid. But for the most exciting, aromatic, intensely flavoured Sauvignon Blanc – gooseberries, asparagus, red peppers, nettles, elderflowers, grass – New Zealand is the place.

SEMILLON

The grape that succumbs to botrytis, or "noble rot", Sémillon brings peachy, nutty fruit flavours, honey and vanilla, to Bordeaux's sweet wines. Blended with Sauvignon Blanc and Chardonnay, or on its own, Sémillon's value as a dry white has really been demonstrated by Australia, with its lime-zest, honeyed flavours and fat character. Age brings an intriguing burnt-toast character.

RIESLING

Perfumed, very floral in character, with a steely flash of acidity and citrus flavours, this is the classic grape of Germany. Aged Riesling develops a unique petrolly aroma. In the cooler regions of Australia, New Zealand and the West Coast of America, those pungent, limey, refreshingly acid flavours, with lots of fruit, come to the fore. A hardy vine that withstands the cold of northern Europe and Canada, it is perfect for late harvesting, yielding luscious, delicately sweet wines, streaked with acidity.

FAR LEFT: *A glass of white wine – its colour alone can vary from the palest of pale to deep straw-gold.*

ABOVE: *Sauvignon Blanc in its homeland of Sancerre, in France's beautiful Loire Valley.*

RIGHT: *Autumn colours the Riesling vineyards above Piesport, on the banks of the Mosel river in Germany.*

RED GRAPE VARIETIES

So-called red grapes can be purple, almost black, or vibrant blue. Like the Syrah, it's the skins that gives the wine its red hue – the juice is pale.

CABERNET SAUVIGNON

Cabernet Sauvignon, the noble red grape of Bordeaux, where it is blended with Merlot and Cabernet Franc, is a full-bodied, tannic grape that ages gracefully. Ripe Cabernet is full of warm, juicy blackcurrants, plums and blackberries, and the warm climes of Australia and Chile yield a note of mint and eucalyptus. Oak brings cigar-box scents and cedary notes to the wine. With age, Cabernet develops a savoury, complex character, with dried fruits, and sometimes dark chocolate.

MERLOT

Merlot is softer and more rounded, with gentle, plummy, sometimes dried-fruit flavours and low tannins. It smooths the edges off Cabernet Sauvignon in a blend. Merlot shares the grassy character of cool-climate Cabernet, notably in New Zealand, and its inherent blackcurrany character. In California and Washington State especially, Merlot has become highly fashionable as a soft, fruity, youthful varietal wine.

PINOT NOIR

Light, low in tannins, and incredibly fussy about how it is treated, at its finest the grape of red Burgundy is a mouthful of fragrant, soft, sweet red fruits – think of strawberries, cherries – when young, maturing to an earthy, pruney, savoury character. In very cool areas, it is delicate, very pale and lightly fruity, but where it's too hot, it turns into boiled jam. Pinot Noir brings a delicacy of aroma and flavour to Champagne and sparkling wines, and the hue to many rosé wines.

SYRAH

Syrah comes from the northern Rhône region of France. Here it can make massive, deep, concentrated wines that smell of damsons, plums and other dark fruits, with a peppery, smoky, even liquorice character, and tannins that allow it to age extremely well. Syrah blends well with other varieties. In Australia, it has become famous as Shiraz. You'll find block-buster, fruity, rich Shirazes, with creamy oak, and gentler, lighter ones, but still with that signature spicy, tarry note.

FAR LEFT: *A glass of red wine – a mouthful can taste of cherries or plums, mint or liquorice, tobacco or chocolate.*

ABOVE: *The chapel set amid vines on the Hill of Hermitage is a landmark of the Rhône, home to the Syrah grape.*

RIGHT: *This painting by Lemoine (1605-1665) captures the true colour of "red" grapes; so often their skins are purple, black, or even blue.*

THE BEST OF THE REST

There are hundreds of varieties of grapes planted in vineyards around the world. Of these, just a handful are internationally recognised, while others enjoy only local repute. There are a number of these characterful, fine grapes well worth remembering when you are buying bottles of wine.

WHITES

Viognier is earning a high reputation around the world for its wonderful apricot and peach flavours, both in southern France and in California, while Alsace's exotic, dusky-pink skinned Gewürztraminer shines out for its spicy, aromatic character, dry and sweet, and its extraordinary likeness to lychees. Pinot Gris, at its best in Alsace, makes fat, spicy, dry wine, and some excellent sweet styles too. As Pinot Grigio in Italy, the best are fresh, fruity, simple dry whites.

The Loire grape, Chenin Blanc, has an impressive versatility, from bone-dry, acid sparkling and still wines – tart and nutty in flavour – to great honeyed, sweet wines. In South Africa, where it is called Steen, Chenin makes easy-drinking wines. Muscat can be dry, sweet, still, sparkling or fortified. Musky-scented and grapey-flavoured when dry, as a sweet wine it transforms into an unctuous, raisiny and treacly blend.

REDS

As Beaujolais, Gamay makes vibrant purple-coloured, fresh, fruity young wine, packed with distinctive red cherry and strawberry jam flavours, and bubble-gum or banana smells from the method of vinification used. Grenache lends spice to southern Rhône blends, and it creates wonderful light strawberry-like reds and rosés, and concentrated, heavy, fruit-rich, oaked wines from old vines, especially in Australia. Spain's finest red grape, Tempranillo, has a light, soft, perfumed summer-fruit style when young; given some age and oak, and blended with Cabernet Sauvignon, it produces more weighty, herby, often gamey characteristics. Sangiovese is the grape of Italy's Chianti, at its best showing rich plum and cherry-stone flavours and high tannins that soften to tobacco-y, elegant maturity. When well-made, California's exclusive Zinfandel has delicious blackberry fruit and peppery flavours, whether light and juicy or weighty, rich and concentrated in style.

FAR LEFT: *A machine harvests Grenache grapes destined for the cave co-operative in Vaucluse, France.*

RIGHT: *The timelessness of a gourmet feast – fresh oysters and chilled white wine in a still life painted by Beert in the sixteenth century.*

BELOW: *A classic springtime sight in California – mustard and vines. These are 100-year-old Zinfandel vines.*

WINEMAKING PROCESSES

There's a kind of magic involved in winemaking. Natural processes are harnessed and exploited, and fabulous things begin to happen.

MAKING WHITE WINE

To make good, fresh-tasting white wine requires care and speed from the moment the grapes are picked. The grape juice should not come into contact with oxygen, as far as possible, otherwise you risk ending up with oxidized wine. (Grapes are easily squashed at the bottom of the picker's basket.)

Arriving at the winery, the grapes are either pressed straight away to separate the juice from the skins, or lightly crushed and then left for up to 24 hours or so before pressing. Leaving the skins and juice together for a *short* time gives extra flavour to the finished wine, but doesn't allow the colour and tannins in the skins to start affecting the juice too, which you don't want in white wines.

The clear-coloured juice is run from the press into the fermentation vats. Old-fashioned wineries may still have concrete tanks; more modern set-ups are equipped with stainless steel tanks. A major benefit of modern tanks is that they can be temperature-controlled: fermenting white wine at cool temperatures keeps that fresh, fruity character in the wine. That's much easier to achieve with today's technology.

MALOLACTIC FERMENTATION

❖ This is a rather scientific-sounding process, but one that makes red wines smooth, and white wines creamy. It refers to the conversion of hard malic acid into soft lactic acid. It's a natural process that happens after the main fermentation and can be prevented, if so desired, by the winemaker. White Burgundy is a typical example of a style of wine that is generally "allowed to go through its malo".

FAR LEFT: *"The Grape Harvest" by Kilmsch.*

ABOVE: *Treading grapes, the crudest form of pressing grapes to release their juice.*

RIGHT: *A more recent method of pressing grapes, this horizontal screw-press is being filled with Muscadet grapes.*

For a deeply-coloured, tannic red, such as California Cabernet, the skins and juice may be left together for up to two weeks; for a lighter-hued red for drinking young, such as a vin de pays Syrah from southern France, it can be five or six days. The juice will then be run off to continue fermenting separately.

FERMENTATION

Walk into a winery at harvest-time and there's a warm, yeasty smell. This is the smell of ferment-ing grape must. Grapes have yeasts on their skins, but these are often insufficient to see the fer-mentation through, so the winemaker will add natural or cultivated yeasts. These act with the fruit sugar and convert it to alcohol, creating heat and giving off CO_2 in the process.

Fermentation ceases when all the sugar has been converted to alcohol, or when the alcohol level reaches about 15 degrees and "stops" the yeasts acting. The winemaker can also choose the cut-off point. The yeasts will die off and fall as sediment to the bottom of the vat. This sediment is known as "lees".

ROSE WINES

❖ Traditionally, the dark skins and pale juice of red grapes are left in contact with each other for up to three days. The pinkish juice is then run off to complete fermentation.

Top-quality white wines are still fermented, or at least part-fermented, in oak barrels. This emphasizes the fruit and gives the wine a subtle vanilla-oak flavour.

MAKING RED WINE

Red grapes destined for red wine are crushed, and the thick pulp (skins, pips, and sometimes stems too) is put into vats or oak barrels for fermentation.

The juice and skins are kept together in mak-ing red wine. As the wine ferments, the colour in the skins leaches into the juice, along with tan-nins, which are important if the wine is to age. This process is called maceration.

MAKING BEAUJOLAIS

❖ Beaujolais is a soft, fruity wine, rich red in colour, but low in tannin. It is made using whole-bunch fermentation, or carbonic maceration. The Gamay grapes are put, uncrushed, into a closed vat and the space left at the top is filled with carbon dioxide. Gradually, the grapes begin to ferment inside their skins until they burst and fermentation continues as normal. Raspberry, red-cherry, banana and bubble-gum aromas and flavours are good signs a wine has been made in this way.

TANNINS

❖ Tannin is a chemical compound in the grape skin that transfers into the juice during fermentation, and then acts as a preservative in red wine. You can tell if a wine is tannic by the furry, dry sensation it leaves on your gums.

FAR LEFT: *A bubbling mass of fermenting Cabernet Sauvignon grapes, vibrant pinky-red in colour.*

LEFT: *These boards keep the "cap", or crust, of grape skins and pips that forms during the process of red winemaking submerged in the fermenting juice.*

IN THE
CELLAR

Certain white wines are delicious when "oaked". Chardonnay is wonderfully susceptible to oak, and Sauvignon Blanc is increasingly aged in oak for a short time particularly in Bordeaux. Ageing fine red wines, such as top Bordeaux, in oak lends a whole new dimension to the wine. It adds distinctive vanilla, smoky toast aromas and flavours, and softens the tannins in the wine as the oak slowly lets in oxygen. The younger the oak used, and the smaller the barrel, the more flavour is imparted to the wine. Visit a cellar in Tuscany, for example, and rows of gleaming new oak barrels will greet you, their sides stained with the red Chianti Classico.

THE ATTRACTION OF AGE

Wines made for drinking young, such as Soave or Vinho Verde, will be bottled and sold as soon as the winemaking has finished. Other wines are designed to be aged, first in oak (6–24 months) and then in the bottle (2– 20 years), before being drunk. For a wine to mature successfully, it needs good quality fruit, tannin, acidity and alcohol.

As a wine ages, the scents and tastes alter, the colour changes, and it develops a mellow, softer character. How long it takes the wine to reach its peak of maturity depends on many factors, not least how the wine is stored.

Cabernet Sauvignon is a good grape variety for ageing. Claret is a traditional choice for claying down for a number of years, as are, more recently, Cabernets from top producers around the world. Italy's Nebbiolo grape from Piedmont also matures well, as does the Syrah of the northern Rhône. Vintage Champagne that is left to age can develop tasty, rich characteristics, while old red Burgundy develops earthy, savoury tones.

Two dry white wines that mature into rich, complex wines in the bottle, with no recourse to oak, are the rich Australian Sémillons and petrolly-flavoured German Rieslings. Sémillon in its guise as sweet Sauternes can mellow into a honeyed richness, and Chenin Blanc from the Loire is often overlooked for its fine aged sweet wine.

FAR LEFT: *Vault-like cellars, here filled with new oak barrels, were built underground for coolness and darkness.*

LEFT: *Oak barrels are made in varying sizes, which has its advantages, as this merry eighteenth-century scene, painted by Cesare, shows.*

ABOVE: *A mix of old and new oak barrels line the narrow corridors of this dim, cool cellar in Spain.*

THE ROLE OF THE WINEMAKER

He used to stay hidden among his barrels, never known to the wine-drinker except by his wares. These days, the winemaker is a high-profile character. Wine-makers from famous Bordeaux châteaux and big Australian and Californian companies alike are now flying the world, leading seminars, consulting, and marketing their wines.

The winemaker has been described variously as the artist, the architect and the scientist of wine. However the role is viewed, the responsibility of the winemaker is to take the grapes and guide them into a particular style.

He or she decides the moment at which the grapes are ready for picking; what the blend of grapes will be to create the best end result; which yeasts to use; what temperature the grapes should ferment at, the percentage of old to new oak, how long the wine spends in each before bottling. These are tremendous responsibilities, and it means that during the harvest and vinification life is hectic and the days are long.

The major producers tend to have vineyard managers, cellar managers, and often winemakers who specialize in particular styles of wine. By contrast, in small, privately-owned wineries the winemaker is likely to be the grower and the cellar master too.

CO-OPERATIVES

A co-operative is a vinification and bottling centre set up by a group of growers, or run as a business to which local grape-growers are contracted. In France, co-ops produce much of the best *vins de pays*. A large proportion of Spain and Portugal's wines are made this way, and South Africa is a notable New World follower of co-operatives.

FLYING WINEMAKERS

Nowadays there are a number of winemakers who, eager to learn more from other countries, travel the world. They make wine in France, Eastern Europe or Italy from September to November, and afterwards fly south to catch the harvest in Argentina, South Africa or Australia in March. This phenomenon has led to a fascinating cross-fertilization of winemaking styles.

FAR LEFT: *Checking the progress of a red wine maturing in oak barrels.*

ABOVE: *Taking a sample of Chardonnay from new oak barrels to see how much longer it should stay there before being bottled.*

RIGHT: *A connoisseur, painted by Crochepierre in 1886, carefully studies the colour of the wine before he drinks.*

WINES AROUND THE WORLD

The winemaking world is generally regarded as consisting of two halves – the Old World and New World. In effect Europe and the Middle East are the Old World, and the rest of the world is the New – even if such a generalization is rather misleading when you think that South Africa, for example, has been making wine since the 1650s.

But what sets the New World countries apart is the wonderful sense of freedom that characterizes their winemaking: the freedom to experiment, to try out new grapes in new areas, creating new styles, using new blends. And the success of the wines has made the Old World look to its laurels. The result is a fantastic and still evolving variety of wine styles to choose from.

SPARKLING WINES

Champagne is France's most northerly wine region. It's the home of a style of fizz against which all others are judged. Champagne is made primarily with a blend of Chardonnay and Pinot Noir grapes, with a percentage of Pinot Meunier in some styles. It can be dry or sweet, and can also be rosé.

Why is Champagne sparkling? A mixture of sugar and yeast, called the *dosage*, is added to fermented wine in a sealed bottle or larger container. This triggers a second fermentation, during which carbon dioxide is released. Trapped in the wine, it takes the form of . . . bubbles. It's known as the *méthode Champenoise*.

Sparkling wines made from Chardonnay and Pinot Noir abound in New Zealand, California and Australia, in particular. Warm sunshine means the grapes are riper, so the style tends to be richer, fruitier, but still elegant. But you don't need to look so far afield for alternatives, such as the semi-sparkling Crémants of Alsace and Burgundy, the Loire Valley's dry or sweet, white or rosé sparkling wines, Italy's low-alcohol, spritzy Asti, and Spain's Cava, made in Penedès.

FAR LEFT: *Bubbles stream up through the sparkling wine to form a "mousse".*

ABOVE: *Making Champagne: the blender mixes a number of different "cuvées", or batches, of wine to create a certain style and flavour.*

RIGHT: *This still life by Josef Mansfeld in 1882 depicts the familiar shape of a Champagne bottle.*

RED WINES

Lovers of traditional fine red wine head for Bordeaux and to Burgundy, the home of the Pinot Noir grape variety. Around the world, winemakers have sought to emulate the elegant, perfumed red Burgundy. Pinot Noir is planted from Spain to New Zealand, Germany to Chile, but perhaps the most famous of the "pretenders" comes from Oregon. An Oregon Pinot Noir caused quite a stir when it triumphed in a comparative tasting of top French and New World wines in 1979.

Cabernet Sauvignon is the noble red grape variety of Bordeaux. It has the tannin to age, and with oak it develops wonderful aromas and flavours. The Bordeaux châteaux blend it with the softer, perfumed Merlot – the second red grape of the region – to create the stylish red wine known as claret.

HALF-WAY HOUSE

❖ Say "Provence", and it still conjures images of onion-coloured wine and fish stew. It's true that southern France does make lots of pink, or rosé, wines, from Languedoc to the southern Rhône, but so does the more northern Loire. You can also enjoy *rosados* in Spain, or taste the fruits of a trend in California for "blush" wines.

Look to California, Chile and Australia in particular and you'll find an abundance of wonderful Bordeaux-style reds. Australia also substitutes Shiraz for Merlot to make a beefier, spicier style.

Closer to home, in southern France, in Italy and in Spain, Cabernet Sauvignon dominates in many red wine styles. Eastern Europe was put on the wine map with Bulgarian Cabernet Sauvignon in the 1980s, while Argentina packs a punch with a hefty style of Cabernet.

REDS THE WORLD OVER

Australia made its mark with the big, spicy Shiraz, a grape known in France's Rhône region as Syrah, and California has a native red grape, Zinfandel. As for softer, fruitier, gentle reds, and vanilla-oaked reds that slip down a treat, these can be found all over the world, from the Loire to Chile. Not to be outdone, South Africa produces fine reds with its own grape, Pinotage. Italy boasts the fine big Piedmontese reds, Barolo and Barbaresco, as well as Chianti, made from Sangiovese (which you can also find in California). Spain's Rioja and Ribera del Duero regions produce sweet-fruited, oaked Tempranillo.

ABOVE LEFT: *The Gamay grape of Beaujolais, making fresh, cherry-fruited wines.*

BELOW LEFT: *Modern wineries are filled with enormous stainless steel vats, used to ferment the wines.*

RIGHT: *Tasting the red wine from barrel.*

CLASSIC REDS

❖ The five red grapes of Bordeaux are as follows: Cabernet Sauvignon; Merlot; Cabernet Franc; Malbec; and Petit Verdot.

WHITE WINES

To the north of Burgundy lies Chablis, where the Chardonnay grape makes a crisp, appley-fruited, usually unoaked white wine. Further south, in the region's Côte d'Or area, the grape is transformed into the creamy-buttery *"grand cru"* elegance of white Burgundy, and is held up as the ultimate expression of the Chardonnay grape.

In North America, the evocatively named Finger Lakes of New York State, as well as the cooler Washington and Oregon, will treat you well with cool, elegant Chardonnays.

The Bordelais were not to be outdone by the Burgundians' skill at both white and red wine-making. Living close to the Atlantic ocean, with all its abundant seafood, the Bordelais needed a complimentary fresh, crisp white wine. This they have in the shape of Sauvignon Blanc, occasionally blended with Sémillon.

Further north, the River Loire has seen centuries of winemaking along its 1000-mile journey through central France, where gooseberryish Sauvignon Blanc now overshadows the classic sweet Chenin Blanc.

Alsace has the wonderfully aromatic Pinot Gris, the rich Pinot Blanc and the spicy Gewürztraminer, while Germany's rivers sweep past famous castles and vineyards where dry and sweet, young and old Rieslings fit for royalty have been made for centuries.

Northern Italy stays with the simpler Pinot Grigio and Soave, while northern Spain has the aromatic Alvariñho and Portugal has the youthful fresh Vinho Verde.

HEAD FOR THE SUN

Feel the warmth of the sun in France's Languedoc region, and taste it in rich, weighty Viognier and fruity *vins de pays*. Follow the sun to Chile, where the classic white grapes of France have been taken and turned into aromatic Sauvignon and dollops of oaky Chardonnay. But it is the New Zealanders who have struck gold with an inimitable style of Sauvignon Blanc all their own, packed with delicious flavours.

POWER-HOUSES

Take the grape of white Burgundy, blend it with sunshine and oak, and what do you have? Big Australian Chardonnays, where ripe tropical fruit and toasty oak flavours are packed into the bottle. A variation on the same theme takes place in California in a delicious blend of rich fruit and spicy, vanilla oak.

FAR LEFT: *Chenin Blanc makes classic sweet wines in the Loire; it is also well-established in South Africa.*

BELOW: *One of England's less common country scenes – mechanical harvesting in a Kent vineyard.*

RIGHT: *Hand-picked Riesling grapes; fine German Rieslings can develop a unique petrolly character with age.*

SWEET AND FORTIFIED WINES

The south bank of the River Garonne in Bordeaux passes the vineyards of Sauternes and Barsac, where autumn mists and botrytis, or "noble rot", descend on the vines and transform Sémillon into a world-class sweet wine.

Hungary drew the attention of Europe's nobility as far back as the seventeenth century with the famous, much-admired sweet wine, Tokaji, made from botrytised grapes.

Travel to Germany and Austria in late November and you may see shrivelled, browned bunches of grapes left dangling on the bare vines. They may look unattractive, but these are destined for classic, sweet white wine. It's risky – it may rain, or turn cold – but these late-harvested grapes are bursting with sugar.

FORTIFIED FLAVOURS

Fly to the other side of the world, to western Victoria in Australia, and you'll find a completely different style of sweet wine. The Rutherglen Liqueur Muscat is rich, sticky, raisiny and fortified. It's rather like drinking heavy fruit cake.

Liqueur Muscat may be made in the southern hemisphere but its ties with the fortified wines of Spain and Portugal are close. Like Madeira and Málaga, Liqueur Muscat is made using the *solera* system. This is a form of blending used by the Spaniards to make sherry in sun-baked Jerez. The solera is a stack of barrels; the bottom one contains the oldest wine while new wine is added to the top one. As wine is drawn out from the bottom barrel, it is replenished with wine from the next one up.

The father of fortified wine is port. This sweet, high-alcohol wine is made in the valley of the River Douro in northern Portugal. It enjoyed great demand as the *digestif* of choice in the nineteenth-century gentlemen's clubs, and is still very popular today as an after-dinner drink.

FAR LEFT: *Three nineteenth-century gentlemen enjoy their digestifs in the library.*

ABOVE: *Five styles of sherry, ranging from the very sweet Pedro Ximénez (left) to the pale, dry fino.*

RIGHT: *The ornate Façon de Venise glass, just one of hundreds of wine glasses designed over the centuries.*

CHAPTER 3

WINE
AT THE
TABLE

LEFT: *A noble family dines, with a very early version of a wine cooler at the bottom left of the picture.*

ABOVE: *"A Steady Hand" after dinner, by Edgar Bundy.*

HOW TO
TASTE

Knowing how to taste – or "assess" – can really enhance your appreciation of wine. Think of it rather as a detective process, of looking, smelling and tasting.

The first thing to look at is the clarity of the wine: it should be bright and clear.

Now look at the wine's colour. Obviously it's either white or red, but take a second look: is it palest white, suggesting a cool-climate, young wine, or is it bright straw-gold, suggesting a warm-climate or oaked wine? The red wine might be ruby, garnet or bright purple. You can pick up clues to a red's age in the colour too. Tip the glass about 45 degrees; a deep-coloured centre and pinkish rim indicate youth; a paler red with an orangey-brown rim speaks of age.

Swirl the wine fairly energetically in the glass (to release the aromas) and then take a sniff or two. A good wine should yield some lovely aromas: try thinking of them in terms of fruity, vegetal and floral, and see what adjectives this inspires.

Now taste it. Swoosh the wine around in your mouth. The first thing you'll notice is any sweetness; your mouth will water if there's lots of acid; and if your gums and teeth feel dry or "furry", that's tannin.

What flavours spring to mind? Again, think of fruit and vegetables – including herbs and spices. Can you taste vanilla, or spice, or smoky toast,

FAR LEFT: *Tipping the glass to check the colour of the wine it contains.*

LEFT: *Sniffing. Aromas can be quite subtle, even elusive; at other times you hardly need to put your nose to the glass.*

RIGHT: *A proud wine-maker takes a merchant down to his cellar for a tasting of a good vintage. By Friedrich Friedlander.*

pointers to oak being used in the winemaking? How does the wine feel in your mouth? Heavy and warm, suggesting higher alcohol, or is it smooth, or perhaps flabby owing to low acidity?

A good wine will leave you with an impression of balance – all those elements working together in harmony to produce a delicious mouthful that leaves you wanting more.

TASTING TIPS
❖ Use a medium-sized tulip-shaped glass. Make sure it has a stem, so that your hand doesn't warm the bowl of the glass and the wine.

❖ Have some white paper to hand to hold the glass over and check the colour.

❖ Try to stay clear of smoke, perfume or other aromas.

❖ Lipstick can really confuse the taste-buds!

SERVING WINE

The ideal place to store wine is in a cool, slightly damp, dark cellar, where the temperature is a constant 13°C/55°F, and where wines can be stored on their sides, undisturbed, in racks.

Not many of us can achieve that, so the next best solution is somewhere that is not too hot, where the temperature doesn't fluctuate too much, and the wine won't be exposed to bright light. A cupboard that you don't need to open often, and in which air can circulate, is a good option.

When it comes to serving the wine, drinking a warm white wine, for instance, is not a pleasant experience. Chill it down, and all those lovely fruity flavours, the crisp acidity or toasty oak character, are revealed. The reverse is true of most red wine: too cold and the fruit is hidden; too warm and the alcoholic punch dominates.

"Room temperature" has become a questionable guide since the invention of central heating and air-conditioning. For those who wish to be precise, here's a guide to serving temperatures:

Champagne/sparkling wine: 5 – 7°C/41 – 45°F
Aromatic/lighter wines: 7 – 8°C/45 – 46°F
Full-bodied/oaked whites: 8 – 10°C/46 – 50°F
Sweet wines: 10°C/50°F
Young/fruity reds: 12 – 14°C/54 – 57°F
Mature/full-bodied reds: 14 – 18°C/57 – 64°F

WINE GLASSES

Holding a fine wine glass is a pleasure in itself. But the design of the glass can also add to the enjoyment of good wine.

❖ Choose plain, clear glass so you can enjoy the colour of the wine.

❖ A long stem prevents the warmth of your hand inadvertently heating up the wine.

❖ A glass that curves in to the rim directs the aromas towards your nose, rather than out into the room.

❖ Use Champagne flutes for sparkling wines. The narrow shape traps the froth, or mousse, keeping the wine bubbly for longer. Make sure the flutes are well rinsed. Any traces of washing-up liquid will kill the bubbles, ruining that wonderful spritzy sensation in the mouth.

Pop white wine in the freezer for 20 minutes, or in a bucket filled with ice, if you haven't had the chance to chill the bottle in advance. Warm up a glass of red wine by cupping it in your hand and helping it to room temperature. Cherish it.

FAR LEFT: *"Vin, femmes et musique", with generous servings of red wine in a large Champagne bowl. By Roehn (1799-1864).*

LEFT: *Wine glasses for different wines, from the Champagne flute and sherry copita, to the deep-bowled red wine glass.*

RIGHT: *The bottle cellar at this world-famous Bordeaux château is filled with older vintages of claret.*

DECANTING WINE

Offering guests a decanter filled with deep-red wine does enhance the sense of theatre.

The ceremony traditionally begins when the wine is brought up from the cellar in advance to bring it to "room temperature". It is stood upright to allow the sediment to drop to the bottom.

The sommelier then holds the bottle neck over a candle flame while decanting. As the last sediment-rich dregs of wine reach the bottle neck, the sommelier can see them and stop pouring. Placing a filter in the top of the decanter catches any stray bits.

The advantage of decanting is that it allows a wine to "breathe". Exposure to oxygen as the wine pours into the decanter allows its aromas and flavours to be released. Decanting younger reds half-an-hour or so ahead of time is fine, but not so with old wines. These are fragile, with little flavour left, and even that half-hour can be too long.

Vintage port, mature red Burgundy and claret, and some big Australian and California Cabernets, still may "throw a sediment", but generally, thanks to modern winemaking methods, few wines *need* decanting. If in doubt, don't decant; just try and be patient when that first glass is poured, and give it a few moments to open up if it needs to.

SAVING AND COOKING WITH WINE

Re-cork your bottle and it will be fine for the next day. Whites should be popped in the fridge. A worthwhile investment is a wine saver, which keeps reds and whites fresh for days. You can also buy special stoppers for Champagne. Myth has it that leaving a silver teaspoon in the neck of the bottle keeps the bubbles inside.

Use leftover wine in cooking. A generous splash of red wine – or sherry or port – in the gravy, or white wine in a creamy sauce or casserole, adds delicious flavours to the dish. Add a dash of sweet wine (if there's any left!) into a fresh fruit salad, or pour "PX" (Pedro Ximénez) Sherry over your vanilla ice cream.

FAR LEFT: *Storing bottles on their sides keeps the corks moist.*

ABOVE: *A quick way of allowing a wine to breathe – pour it from the bottle into a jug, and then back again.*

RIGHT: *A cut-glass decanter and pair of wine glasses form part of "A Christmas Table", by Eloise Stannard.*

MATCHING FOOD AND WINE

Matching food and wine effectively can transform both and make any meal a triumphant experi- ence. It can also be fun. Don't be put off by the smorgasbord of wine styles and recipes that there are to choose from.

The old rule of thumb, "White wine with Fish, Red wine with Meat" makes a good basis from which to work, but be prepared to experiment; that way you'll discover some wonderful combinations. Take a few moments to consider the flavours in you plan to eat, and look for a wine that will complement them.

It's really a question of balance. You may be serving fish or meat, but the herbs, spices and sauce all contribute to the overall taste of the dish. Perhaps it's a simple dish, in which case a more complex wine can be allowed to shine. Alternatively, it may be a "melting pot" of rich flavours, so that a straightforward wine will be a relief on the taste-buds.

Otherwise, if you have a particularly fine bot- tle, why not start with the wine, and find a recipe that has flavours in it to flatter the wine? Or sim- ply throw caution to the wind and follow a whim; it may turn out to be perfect.

A safe guide is to serve white before red, light wines before heavier wines, dry before sweet. Put young before old, and make sure that the better

of two wines comes second. Think of it as you would prepare a menu: more often than not the more delicate dish precedes the richer, more flavoured dish; it's the same with the wine.

CLASSIC COMBINATIONS

❖ Think of oaked Chardonnay with smoked salmon, port and Stilton. Champagne with smoked salmon and scrambled eggs is the ultimate brunch, and *foie gras* with Sauternes is sheer luxury. The pleasure these give should inspire you to discover other equally delicious matches.

FAR LEFT: *Drawing the cork on a bottle of fizz to start the meal in style.*

ABOVE: *Sweet, or dessert wines can add a new dimension of interest and flavour to the final course.*

RIGHT: *A decanter of wine on the table, set for an informal lunch. Painting by Louise Abbema (1858-1927).*

PARTNERSHIPS WITH FOOD

Start the meal in style with sparkling wine, which complements a whole variety of flavours, or try a chilled fino sherry with tapas-style entrées.

LIGHT WHITE WINES

Light, crisp, dry and unoaked whites such as Loire or Bordeaux Sauvignon Blanc, or unoaked Spanish whites, emphasize the texture and flavour of crunchy green salads.

Try Chablis or white Bordeaux with pasta in creamy sauces. They cut through the richness of the cream deliciously.

Serve delicate white fish with Italian Soave, cool-climate Sauvignons or gently flavoured whites from Spain's Galicia.

OFF-DRY OR AROMATIC WHITES

Riesling, Gewürztraminer and Tokay-Pinot Gris, from Alsace and Germany, or the Oregon Pinot Blanc, all have a balance of good acidity and a touch of sweetness which make them ideal partners for Thai-style dishes.

GENTLY FRUITY WHITES

Still and sparkling white wines work very well with eggs. Unoaked Chardonnay – French or Italian, especially – is a treat with omelettes and quiches, for example.

Like Chardonnay, Sauvignon Blanc is a great food wine. It strikes a wonderful chord with herbs – make sure they are fresh herbs! Tangy Sauvignon Blanc (led by New Zealand, but look also to Chile and South Africa) works wonders with a plate of fresh asparagus.

Sauvignon is also the saviour when it comes to tomato sauces. It copes admirably with the acid tomato that can flatten many wines.

RICH AND OAKED WHITES

Partner firm, meaty fish – such as sea bream or turbot – with characterful, elegant, oaked wines, for example Chardonnays, white Rhônes and Australian Sémillons.

FAR LEFT: *White wine is a good bet when serving an egg dish.*

BELOW: *Flatter fish in rich or creamy sauces with less demanding white wines.*

RIGHT: *Along France's Atlantic coast, fresh fish and seafood are traditionally served with the local, dry, crisp white wines.*

Pink-fleshed salmon is a treat with ripe Chardonnays and Rieslings. Smoked salmon is rich, smooth and often quite "sweet". Flatter that luxurious taste and serve rich Alsace Pinot Blanc or Tokay-Pinot Gris, or fine, creamy-oaked Chardonnays from Burgundy or California.

The white grape Viognier can be quite fat and rich, and makes a good sparring partner with spicy, creamy and curry-style dishes.

RED WINES

Many people do crave a red wine with their main course, whether it's beef or fish. There are plenty to choose from.

LIGHT, FRUITY REDS

If you feel like drinking (young) Pinot Noir or dry rosé, this is the time to serve salmon or tuna, or meaty white fish.

Duck and goose are fatty birds. To match these you need wines with good acidity and lots of flavour. Chianti Classico and New Zealand Pinot Noir will provide just that combination.

Roasted vegetables in tomato sauce, or pasta with a tomato-based sauce, are a treat with fruity young reds like Beaujolais or young Italian reds made from the Sangiovese or Barbera grapes.

Believe it or not, a mild tomato-based curry goes down a treat with the Spanish red grape variety, Tempranillo.

FULL FRUITY REDS

Serving roast chicken or turkey and stuffing? Claret and the Cabernet-Merlot blends of Australia, New Zealand and California, as well as Pinot Noir and red Rioja, are the styles to look for. Pork and veal suit the savoury, fruity character of Italy's reds, especially Valpolicella.

Why does spaghetti carbonara ruin a good glass of Cabernet Sauvignon? It's the eggs.

Cabernet is a tannic grape, and eggs bring out the tannin in red wine, leaving a metallic, dry taste – in fact, rather like spinach and cream.

Rich, dark, meaty casseroles demand the savoury, rich flavours of Italian reds from the regions of Chianti and Piedmont.

The traditional partner for beef is claret. But think of the noble grape of Bordeaux, Cabernet Sauvignon, which is now planted around the world, and there are plenty of alternatives from the Pacific Northwest of America to Bulgaria.

ABOVE: *Chicken in red wine? The answer's simple – enjoy a red wine with it.*

ABOVE: *Pork cooked with Masala and served with an Italian Dolcetto.*

TOP RIGHT: *The classic – steak and red wine.*

RIGHT: *Serve a Tempranillo-based Spanish red with this dish of chicken and chorizo.*

Lamb is a real winner with Cabernet, too. Or do as the Spanish do, and serve roast lamb with a red Ribera del Duero, made from the Tempranillo grape.

SPICY AND MATURE REDS

For a really punchy combination to enjoy with hot, spicy dishes, ask for a California Zinfandel, Australian Shiraz or southern French Grenache.

Game is traditionally served with mature red Burgundy, in other words Pinot Noir. The more

"gamey" the meat, the richer, more full-bodied the wine can be – for example a Rhône red or an older Rioja.

Big, mature reds are well suited to venison. Spicy wines also work well: again try Shiraz, Zinfandel or Grenache.

THE FINAL COURSES

Serving cheese *before* pudding is not just a strange French tradition. It's very practical. You can mop up the dry wines before the pudding and the sweet wines arrive.

The key is to choose cheeses to go with the wine. Tannic, heavily oaked wines are not cheese-friendly; those with good acidity are.

Camembert is very tasty with fresh, fruity reds or light, crisp whites. Finish up mature, fruity reds with a chunk of Farmhouse Cheddar.

A couple of classic and delicious combinations to round off the meal in style are Roquefort with Sauternes (a botrytised sweet wine that contrasts sublimely with the salty cheese), and Stilton with tawny port (a high-alcohol, fortified style that stands up to the strong blue flavours).

LEFT: The citrus-tang of lemon tart meets its match in late-harvest wines.

RIGHT: Add the finishing touch to a smooth chocolate log with a sweet Muscat.

BELOW: Vin Santo, traditionally served with hard almond biscuits ... just dip them in.

SWEET WINES

Balance the sweetness and tartness in fruit desserts with light, "late-harvest" or Spätlese wines, especially Rieslings from Germany. Botritised wines or sweet sparkling wines such as Sauternes, sweet Vouvray and demi-sec Champagne cope admirably with eggs and cream.

Chocolate-lovers needn't despair. Open a bottle of sweet Muscat with chocolate tortes, botrytised wines with chocolate sauces, or Asti with chocolate mousse.

Savour a tawny or vintage port as you crack a handful of nuts to round off the meal.